Contents

An American Princess

On the sunny afternoon of May 19, 2018, in St. George's Chapel at Windsor Castle, a new princess joined the British royal family. American actress Meghan Markle lived out a fairy-tale dream by marrying her very own Prince Charming—Prince Harry, sixth in line to be king of England.

The pair met on a blind date in July 2016. They kept their relationship quiet for a few months, but it wasn't long until Meghan was meeting the royal family and receiving attention from the press. They announced their engagement in November 2017.

The excitement around Harry and Meghan's wedding was felt all over the world. Only about 600 people were invited to the wedding, including celebrities, members of the royal family, and friends of the bride and groom. More than 2,600 people were invited to view the wedding arrivals on the grounds of Windsor Castle. As many as 100,000 more people lined the roadway leading up to the castle. Billions more watched hours of coverage in countries around the world!

Guest Gallery

David Furnish and Sir Elton John

Oprah Winfrey

Victoria and David Beckham

Amal and George Clooney

Serena Williams and Alexis Ohanian

Sabrina Dhowre and Idris Elba

The Queen's Arrival

As Queen Elizabeth II drove up to Harry and Meghan's wedding, the crowd was stunned to see her husband, Prince Philip, the Duke of Edinburgh, with her. Weeks earlier, the 96-year-old prince had undergone surgery. Many didn't expect him to be well enough to attend. Philip and Harry are very close, and his grandfather's age was one reason Harry wanted his wedding to happen quickly.

Queen Elizabeth and Prince Philip were the last to arrive to the church before the bride. The queen wore a lime green coat over a floral print dress, making a fashion statement as soon as she exited the car.

Since Harry is sixth in line for the crown, he had to ask his grandmother, the queen, for permission to marry Meghan. Meghan wasn't raised in the Church of England, is biracial, and has been married before—all reasons that in the past may have stopped the queen. However, Queen Elizabeth formally granted Harry's engagement request in March 2018.

The Bridal Party

Kate Middleton, the Duchess of Cambridge, accompanied two of her children to the chapel for Harry and Meghan's wedding. She wore a pale yellow dress made by designer Alexander McQueen and a hat made by Philip Treacy. Kate wasn't part of the bridal party, but took her seat in the quire, or choir, of St. George's Chapel. This part of the chapel is nearest to the altar and where the bride and groom's closest family and friends were seated.

Prince George was one of four pageboys, and Princess Charlotte one of six bridesmaids who walked with Meghan down the aisle of St. George's Chapel. The ten children taking part in the wedding were between the ages of 2 and 7.

Traditionally in royal weddings, the pageboys and bridesmaids are all part of the royal family. Harry and Meghan broke with tradition and each chose children of friends and family who were important to them.

Prince Charles and the Duchess of Cornwall

Harry's father and future king of England, Prince Charles, Duke of Wales, arrived with his wife, Camilla Parker-Bowles, Duchess of Cornwall. Camilla is Prince Harry and Prince William's stepmother. She married Charles in 2005.

Over the years, Prince Harry and Prince William have developed a close and loving relationship with Camilla, recognizing how happy she has made their father. Prince Harry once said in an interview, "William and I love her to bits."

Harry's mother, Diana, Princess of Wales, married Charles in 1981. About 750 million people around the world watched their wedding on TV! Charles and Diana officially ended their marriage in 1996, and Diana died in a car accident the following year. Harry was only 12 years old.

From the start, Harry honored his mother's memory in his wedding plans. Meghan's engagement ring includes two diamonds from Diana's jewelry collection. Her veil was long, like Diana's. Harry also picked Diana's favorite flower, white forget-me-nots, for Meghan to carry in her bouquet.

Brothers in Blues

Prince Harry rode to the church with his older brother and best man Prince William, the Duke of Cambridge and second in line to be king of England. Together, they walked past the crowds around St. George's Chapel, waving to the many onlookers as they made their way inside where the wedding ceremony would be held.

Harry and William both wore the navy blue uniform of the Blues and Royals. Harry served in this regiment of the military for 10 years, including two tours of duty in Afghanistan. Queen Elizabeth gave her blessing for Harry and William to wear this uniform to the wedding.

Harry wore a pilot's wing on the left side of his coat. The badge symbolizes the time he spent as a pilot in the Army Air Corps. He also wore medal ribbons representing his time in Afghanistan, the knighthood granted to him by the queen, the queen's golden jubilee, and the queen's diamond jubilee. William wore golden braids to show his membership in the Order of the Garter.

*On her wedding day, Meghan rode to
St. George's Chapel with her mother,
Doria Ragland.*

The First Look

The bride was the last to arrive at St. George's Chapel. As she got ready to enter the chapel, one of the biggest royal wedding secrets was finally revealed—the wedding dress! Meghan wore a simple, elegant wedding dress designed by Claire Waight Keller, who is the first female artistic director of the famous fashion house Givenchy.

Meghan also wore a tiara and a veil. She borrowed the tiara from Queen Elizabeth, and it originally belonged to the queen's grandmother, Queen Mary. Meghan's long veil featured flowers from each of the 53 countries of the Commonwealth—a group of countries that are loyal to the British royal family. The veil also featured the flower that grows where Harry and Meghan live at Kensington Palace, as well as the official flower of Meghan's home state of California.

Meghan's veil was so long that she needed help carrying it! Twin brothers Brian and John Mulroney—the sons of one of Meghan's best friends—helped carry her veil as she walked.

"*The wedding will be a family event.*"

-Spokesperson for the Royal Family

Here Comes the Bride

A bride's father often walks her down the aisle at her wedding. However, Meghan's father, Thomas Markle, had heart surgery only days before the wedding, so he couldn't travel to England to walk her down the aisle.

Meghan made the first part of her journey up the stairs of the chapel and down the long aisle on her own. This was seen by many as a bold statement. It was reported that she was the first bride at a British royal wedding to walk down the aisle alone. Then, she was met by Harry's father, Prince Charles, who walked with her for the rest of the way.

Harry stood at the end of the aisle, waiting for the woman he was about to marry. In Britain, a groom traditionally waits to look at his bride until she's standing next to him. Harry didn't want to wait to see Meghan, so he turned around to watch her make her big entrance.

A Modern Wedding

The walk down the aisle wasn't the only part of the wedding that broke from tradition. Although Harry and Meghan said traditional wedding vows and many parts of the church service were traditional, the wedding ceremony also had many modern elements. It also celebrated Meghan's African American heritage. For example, in addition to traditional music, the wedding also featured a gospel choir. The Kingdom Choir performed "Stand By Me" and "Amen/This Little Light of Mine."

The modern and youthful spirit of the ceremony was also reflected in another musical choice: 19-year-old cello player Sheku Kanneh-Mason. In 2016, he became the first black musician to win the famous BBC Young Musician of the Year competition.

The wedding rings also provided a twist on tradition. Many men in Harry's family, including his brother William, don't wear a wedding ring. Harry, however, chose to wear one.

Words of Wisdom

"There's power in love to show us the way to live."

Those powerful words about love were spoken by Bishop Michael Bruce Curry. He was chosen to speak at the royal wedding, and his heartfelt words touched people around the world. Bishop Curry is the head of the Episcopal Church in the United States, and he talked about important parts of American history, including the civil rights movement. Bishop Curry shared these words from the civil rights leader Dr. Martin Luther King Jr. at the royal wedding:

"We must discover the power of love, the redemptive power of love. And when we do that, we will make of this old world a new world, for love is the only way."

A New Chapter Begins

When the wedding ceremony was over, Harry and Meghan were officially husband and wife. They also received new royal titles: Duke and Duchess of Sussex. Harry and Meghan then walked out of the chapel together. They even shared a kiss in front of the crowds waiting outside!

Following the wedding, the couple took a carriage ride through the town of Windsor. People from around the world lined the streets to see them and to cheer as Harry and Meghan waved from the carriage.

The royal wedding of Prince Harry and Meghan Markle marked the beginning of a new era in the special relationship between the United Kingdom and the United States. It also marked the beginning of a new chapter in this modern fairy tale.

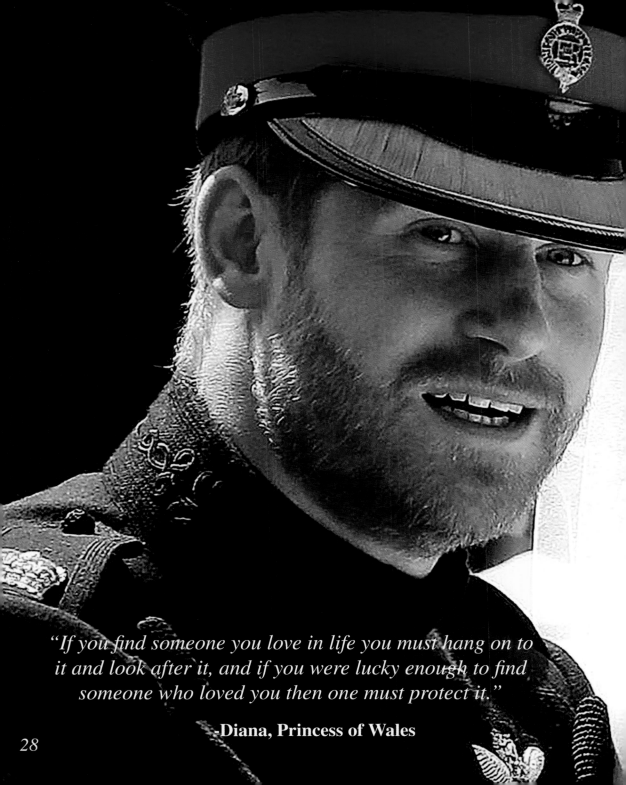

"If you find someone you love in life you must hang on to it and look after it, and if you were lucky enough to find someone who loved you then one must protect it."

-Diana, Princess of Wales

Shown here is one of the official royal wedding portraits taken to honor the special occasion.

Index

Published in 2018 by Enslow Publishing, LLC.
101 W. 23rd Street, Suite 240, New York, NY 10011
Copyright © 2018 by Enslow Publishing

Editor: Kerri O'Donnell
Book Design: Rachel Rising

Photo Credits: Cover BEN STANSALL/Contributor/AFP/Getty Images; Cover, pp. 1, 3, 4, 5, 7, 9, 11, 13, 17, 21, 23, 25, 27, 32 (background) Destinyweddingstudio; pp. 2, 4, (Sir Elton John) (Oprah) 5 (Idris Elba), 6, 8, 16, 20, 22, 24, 26 WPA Pool/Pool/Getty Images Entertainment/Getty Images; pp. 4, (the Beckhams)12 Pool/Samir Hussein/Contributor/WireImages/Getty Images; p. 5 (the Clooneys) Max Mumby/Indigo/Contributor/ Getty Images Entertainment/Getty Images; p. 5 (Serena Williams) IAN WEST/Contributor/ AFP/Getty Images; p. 6 GARETH FULLER/Contributor/AFP; p. 10 ALASTAIR GRANT/Contributor/AFP/Getty Images; pp. 14,15 OLI SCARFF/ Contributor/AFP/Getty Images; pp. 18, 19 OWEN HUMPHREYS/Contributor/AFP/Getty Images; pp. 28, 29 AARON CHOWN/Contributor/AFP/Getty Images; pp. 30, 31 Handout/Getty Images Publicity/Getty Images.

Cataloging-in-Publication Data
Names: Kawa, Katie. | Rajczak Nelson, Kristen.
Title: The royal wedding of Prince Harry and Meghan Markle: a special relationship / Katie Kawa and Kristen Rajczak Nelson.
Description: New York : Enslow Publishing, 2018. | Includes index.
Identifiers: ISBN 9781978506992 (pbk.) | ISBN 9781978506985 (library bound) | ISBN 9781978506978 (ebook)
Subjects: LCSH: Harry, Prince, Duke of Sussex, 1984---Juvenile literature. | Meghan, Duchess of Sussex, 1981---Juvenile literature. | Marriages of royalty and nobility--Great Britain--Juvenile literature.
Classification: LCC DA591.A45 K39 2018 | DDC 941.086092--dc23

Manufactured in the United States of America
CPSIA Compliance Information: Batch #CS18ENS For further information contact Rosen Publishing, New York, New York at 1-800-237-9932.